Getting Around

By Plane

Cassie Mayer

Heinemann
LIBRARY

www.heinemann.co.uk/library
Visit our website to find out more information about **Heinemann Library** books.

To order:
☎ Phone 44 (0) 1865 888066
🖷 Send a fax to 44 (0) 1865 314091
💻 Visit the Heinemann Bookshop at www.heinemann.co.uk/library to browse our catalogue and order online.

First published in Great Britain by Heinemann Library, Halley Court, Jordan Hill, Oxford OX2 8EJ, part of Harcourt Education. Heinemann is a registered trademark of Harcourt Education Ltd.

Editorial: Tracey Crawford, Cassie Mayer, Dan Nunn, and Sarah Chappelow
Design: Jo Hinton-Malivoire
Picture Research: Tracy Cummins
Production: Duncan Gilbert

Originated by Chroma Graphics (Overseas) Pte. Ltd
Printed and bound in China by South China Printing Company

13 digit ISBN 978 0 431 18217 9 (hardback)

11 10 09 08 07 06
10 9 8 7 6 5 4 3 2 1

13 digit ISBN 978 0 431 18321 3 (paperback)

11 10 09 08 07
10 9 8 7 6 5 4 3 2 1

British Library Cataloguing in Publication Data
Mayer, Cassie
Getting around by plane
1.Flight - Juvenile literature 2.Aeronautics, Commercial - Juvenile literature
I.Title
387.7

Acknowledgements
The publishers would like to thank the following for permission to reproduce photographs:
Alamy p. **21** (Jean Van Straten); Corbis pp. **4** (Macduff Everton), **5** (Stephanie Maze), **6** (Todd Gipstein), **7** (Anthony Bannister/Gallo Images), **9** (Richard Hamilton Smith), **11** (George Hall), **13** (Royalty Free), **14** (George Hall), **15** (Kevin Fleming), **18** (George Hall), **19** (Jeff Vanuga), **20** (George B. Diebold), **22** (Mark Hamilton/zefa), **23** (Anthony Bannister/Gallo Images), **23** (Royalty Free), **23** (Royalty Free); Getty Images pp. **8** (Banagan), **10** (Gurzinski), **12** (Harvey), **16** (Melford), **17** (Melford), **23** (Harvey).

Cover image of a Stinson Station Wagon aircraft used with permission of Jim Sugar/Corbis. Back cover image of an MD-11 reproduced with permission of George Hall/Corbis.

Every effort has been made to contact copyright holders of any material reproduced in this book. Any omissions will be rectified in subsequent printings if notice is given to the publishers.

The paper used to print this book comes from sustainable resources.

Contents

Getting around by plane

Every day people move from
place to place.

Some people move by plane.

What planes carry

Some planes carry passengers.

cargo

Some planes carry cargo.

How planes fly

engine

Planes have engines to help them fly.

wing

Planes have wings to help them fly.

Planes take off on runways.

Planes land on runways.

Who works on planes?

Pilots fly planes all over the world.

Flight attendants help passengers on planes.

Where planes fly

Planes fly over cities.

Planes fly over the country.

Planes fly over mountains.

Some planes can land on water.

Some planes can land on ships.

Some planes help fight fires.

Planes take you to many places.

And planes can take you home.

Plane vocabulary

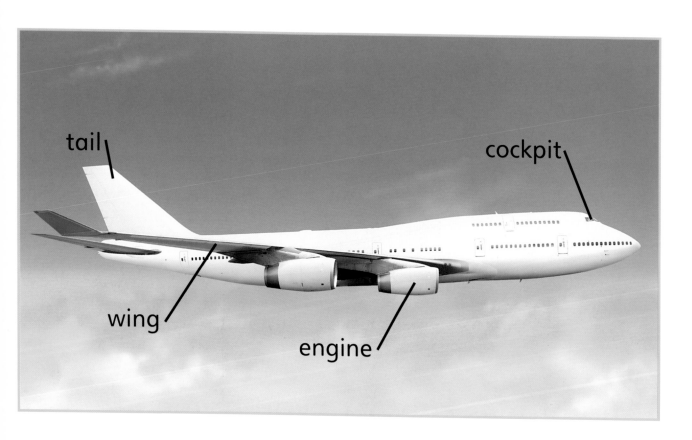

tail

cockpit

wing

engine

Picture glossary

 **cargo** things taken from one place to another

 **flight attendant** person who helps people during a flight

 **passenger** person who flies on a plane

 **pilot** person who flies a plane

Index

Notes to Parents and Teachers
Before reading
Talk about going on a plane journey. Where did they go? Where did they sit? What did they see? Talk about the engine, the wings, the cockpit, the tail, and the cabin.
Talk about people who work on planes: the pilot and the flight attendants.

After reading
Tell the children to pretend to be planes. They should use their arms as wings. Talk about how a plane takes off from the runway, flies through the air, and lands. Talk about how pilots follow signals directing them to the terminal building. Provide small bats or cut out card paddles and let a child give instructions e.g. Come forward, Go left, Go right, Stop. Make a paper aeroplane by folding a sheet of paper to create a nose and wings. See whose plane flies the furthest.
To the tune of "London Bridge is Falling Down", sing "The aeroplane goes up, up, up". Repeat the "up, up, up" and finish with "In the sky". Other verses could be "The aeroplane can loop the loop"; "The aeroplane is coming down".